D1706580

A HEART FOR GOD:

Purposed and United

HANNAH B. KING

ACKNOWLEDGMENTS

I want to thank God for all that He did to put this book together. Through this study, He has drawn me closer to Himself and helped me strengthen my walk with Him.

I also want to thank all of those that have helped me make this book a reality. I have felt God's leading to put some of my Bible study material into print for a long time, but wasn't sure where to begin. My mom encouraged me to "just start." Once I did, God gave me several people that helped move the process along very quickly.

Thank you to my dad and several dear friends who helped me proofread and edit. Thank you to Elikah Basilan for the cover and the formatting work that went into this book.

You have all helped to make something God put on my heart become something real that I can hold in my hands.

INTRODUCTION

Keep thy heart with all diligence; for out of it are the issues of life.
(Proverbs 4:23)

The heart is one's innermost character. The Bible uses the word *heart* to reference our inner man, our mind, our thinking. Our heart is where decisions are made.

God tells us in Jeremiah 17:9 that

> **The heart is deceitful above all things, and desperately**
> **wicked: who can know it?**

God knows that our hearts are deceitful and if we listen to our heart – our way of thinking – we will follow the wrong path. God wants us to *keep* our heart: we must put safeguards in place so that when it comes time to make a decision, we will follow God's best for our lives and not follow our own desires.

What an amazing thing it is that God does not simply tell us to protect our heart, but that He also tells us how to do so according to His Word! And it doesn't stop there – God will help us. God wants to search our hearts for us and lead us in the right way. In Psalm 139:23-24 David says,

(23) Search me, O God, and know my heart: try me, and know my thoughts: (24) And see if there be any wicked way in me, and lead me in the way everlasting.

Over the past couple of years, I have been taking special notice of every time the word *heart* is listed in the Bible. I take the time to use a red or pink pen and draw a small heart around the word. I'm amazed at how many times I've reread a chapter and found that I missed a *heart*. Even after I thought I may have marked them all, God is showing me that I will never be done learning about what He wants for my heart.

The following lessons have come out of my personal devotion time. As God pointed out a specific instance in His Word that *heart* was mentioned, He led me to do some extra study. I believe that studying what God wants for my heart has helped me to draw closer to Him and to strengthen some areas in my life. My prayer is that these studies will be a help and a blessing to you.

PART ONE

A PURPOSED HEART

But Daniel purposed in his heart that he would not defile himself with the portion of the king's meat, nor with the wine which he drank: therefore he requested of the prince of the eunuchs that he might not defile himself. (Daniel 1:8)

Daniel and several young people have been taken out of their home in Judah into captivity in Babylon. King Nebuchadnezzar has given instructions that they are to be fed from the king's meat – the best they have to offer. These young men are to be taught and instructed in the way of the Chaldeans. They have a lot to learn, and a man, the prince of the eunuchs, is in charge of seeing that they stay healthy and learn everything that the king has instructed. His job is to make sure that this group of young men is ready to stand before the king at the appointed time.

Daniel had a decision to make – he knew he could not eat of the king's meat; but that was what his instructions were. This meat could have been meat that had been offered to idols, but most likely it was meat that the Jews would consider unclean, or had blood in it, which was against Jewish law.

Therefore I said unto the children of Israel, No soul of you shall eat blood, neither shall any stranger that sojourneth among you eat blood. (Leviticus 17:12)

(3) Thou shalt not eat any abominable thing. (4) These are the beasts which ye shall eat: the ox, the sheep, and the goat, (5) The hart, and the roebuck, and the fallow deer, and the wild goat, and the pygarg, and the wild ox, and the chamois. (6) And every beast that parteth the hoof, and cleaveth the cleft into two claws, and cheweth the cud among the beasts, that ye shall eat. (7) Nevertheless these ye shall not eat of them that chew the cud, or of them that divide the cloven hoof; as the camel, and the hare, and the coney: for they chew the cud, but divide not the hoof; therefore they are unclean unto you. (8) And the swine, because it divideth the hoof, yet cheweth not the cud, it is unclean unto you: ye shall not eat of their flesh, nor touch their dead carcase. (Deuteronomy 14:3-8)

For Daniel, there was something about this meat that he knew would violate what God wanted him to do in his life, and he now has a choice to make. He could eat the king's meat, regardless of the fact that it was something he knew was against what God had said. Or he could take a stand for what he knew was right.

Should he "go with the flow" and just eat this meat because it was what he was instructed to do? After all, he's been taken captive and has no say in his decisions anymore, right? Should he follow the crowd and do what he's told – keep the peace? Should he take a stand and make a decision that is opposite of what everyone else may do? Should he do what he knows God would have him do?

Think for a moment of the fear that may have been present when he made his decision. What would everyone think? What would be the consequences of not obeying the king's wishes? Would he end up standing for right alone?

Despite everyone else, despite any fear he may have had, Daniel made a decision for himself. He decided that he would not eat the king's meat. This meant asking for special consideration from the prince of the eunuchs. This meant asking to have a different set of rules applied to himself. He didn't know what the consequences of asking would be; but he knew that he could not follow God completely if he did not make this decision.

We each have a decision to make. Not about eating the king's meat – there are no scriptural laws today that restrict the types of meat we can and cannot eat. However, we have to decide if we are going to follow what we desire for our life, what the world says is acceptable; or we have to decide to follow what God says is right in His Word.

Sometimes it is easy to follow the crowd. Maybe you have a close friend or even a relative that likes to plan special events (birthday parties, family reunions, etc.) on Sundays because "it's convenient for our schedules." Maybe you will be offered a promotion at work if you put in extra hours on the weekend. Maybe it's a topic of conversation in the break room at work. How can you choose what you know is right?

We are offered choices every day. Some might be major choices: school/ degree, career, relationship. To make these types of choices we know we need to seek counsel from the Word of God. We look to the Bible and get counsel from godly advisors to make big decisions.

But what about choices we don't even realize we're making – maybe because it's a habit, something we've given in to for so long we don't even realize we are choosing that specific option? Following are some examples (and this is definitely not an exhaustive list) of choices we make every day.

Forgiveness – Bitterness
Holding Our Tongue – Gossip
Harsh Words – Kind, Gracious Words
Giving of Self – Selfishness
Tithing – Holding On To Our Money
Encouraging Someone – Discouraging Someone
Grumpiness – Joy
Complaining – Praising
Worrying – Trusting
Stubborn – Submissive
Witnessing – Giving Excuses
Hard Work – Laziness

In each example, we know what the wrong choice would be and what the right choice would be. Are we going to allow the world, family, friends, circumstances, to sway us to follow them? Are we going to stand our ground and do what God wants?

How did Daniel get to the place where he *purposed in his heart?* He made a decision and he kept it. He did not waver. It was not a sometimes decision. It was an all-the-time decision.

The word *purposed* comes from a Hebrew root word that means to put, place, set, appoint, make, fix, determine, establish; to be set.[i]

The Hebrew word that is translated in Daniel 1:8 as *purposed*, is actually used 585 times in the Old Testament. It is translated into various English words such as *put* (155x), *make* (123x), *set* (119x), *lay* (54x), *appoint* (19x), *give* (11x), *set up* (10x), *consider* (8x) – and several more.[ii]

What do all of these words have in common? They are all actions! Every decision you make is not simply a decision in your mind: "This is what I should do." It requires action. Your decision means very little if there are no actions to make you follow through with that decision.

YOUR DECISION MEANS VERY LITTLE IF THERE ARE NO ACTIONS TO MAKE YOU FOLLOW THROUGH WITH THAT DECISION.

How did Daniel purpose in his heart? How did he make a decision in his mind, "This is what God wants. This is what I'm going to do," and then keep that decision? Daniel made the right choice despite any possible ridicule or fear. But he did not just make a decision – he put his decision into action.

If we are going to have a purposed heart, we must have some actions in our life that help us keep our decisions for God.

Let's look at four different places in the Bible where the Hebrew word for *purposed* is translated. This will help us learn principles about daily actions that we can do to keep us living with a purposed heart – a decision to live according to God's way.

1 - Make God Your Trust

Blessed is that man that maketh the LORD his trust, and respecteth not the proud, nor such as turn aside to lies. (Psalm 40:4)

Maketh is the same Hebrew root word as *purposed*.

Trust is an assured reliance on the character, ability, strength, or truth of someone or something[iii]. The Strong's Concordance gives the definition of trust as "the object of your confidence."[iv]

What is your confidence in? You can decide you are going to trust God to handle every circumstance, because of who He is. Every time you have a choice, if you are deciding to do what God says, you will have to make God your trust.

You will never keep any decision to take a stand for God, to do the right thing, if you don't trust Him: if you don't trust that God is who He says He is; and that He can handle any problem that might come into your life.

Maybe you are struggling with doubt. You aren't sure if God can handle your problems. The good news is that you can learn to trust Him more. In her song "'Tis So Sweet to Trust in Jesus,"[v] Louisa M.R. Stead wrote:

'Tis so sweet to trust in Jesus, Just to take Him at His Word;
Just to rest upon His promise; Just to know, "Thus saith the Lord."
Yes, 'tis sweet to trust in Jesus, Just from sin and self to cease;
Just from Jesus simply taking Life and rest, and joy and peace.
Jesus, Jesus, how I trust Him! How I've proved Him o'er and o'er!
Jesus, Jesus, precious Jesus! O for grace to trust Him more!

How do you learn to make God your trust? Psalm 40:1-4 gives us the answer.

(1) I waited patiently for the LORD; and he inclined unto me, and heard my cry. (2) He brought me up also out of an horrible pit, out of the miry clay, and set my feet upon a rock, and established my goings. (3) And he hath put a new song in my mouth, even praise unto our God: many shall see it, and fear, and shall trust in the LORD. (4) Blessed is that man that maketh the LORD his trust, and respecteth not the proud, nor such as turn aside to lies.

HE HEARS:

First, realize that He hears (v.1). You can trust God because He hears you. When no one else understands the trial you are facing, the difficulty of the decision before you, you can pour out your heart to God. He will hear your prayers.

HE DELIVERS:

Second, realize that He delivers (v.2). God delivers first through salvation. Where would you be without Christ as your Savior? Where would you be if God didn't freely offer His grace. But His deliverance only begins with salvation. At salvation, He delivers us from an eternity separated from Him, condemned

THERE IS NO PROBLEM YOU CAN FACE THAT HE CANNOT OVERCOME.

to hell. After salvation, He continues to deliver us daily from trials and temptations. There is no problem you can face that He cannot overcome.

HE GIVES JOY:

Third, realize that He gives joy (v.3). No matter how difficult the circumstances are that you are facing, He can still give you joy. There is always a reason to praise Him. He wants us to praise Him all the time, but He also gives us reason to praise Him. Even if everything in your life seems to be falling apart, God is still with you. That fact alone should cause you to sing in praise to Him.

Rejoice in the Lord alway: and again I say Rejoice.
(Philippians 4:4)

YOU TRUST:

Fourth, realize that you can trust (v.4). When you take the time to dwell on the fact that God hears your cries to Him, He can deliver you no matter the circumstance, and He can give joy in the darkest of times, you realize that you have a God you can trust. He is not a God "far away" with little or no input in your life. He is near and able to be the object of your confidence.

You can have an assured reliance on the truth of Who God is.

He hears, He delivers, He gives joy – your job is simply to trust. You can take God at His word: "Okay, God, You said You would provide for this need; I am going to trust that You will"; "God, I don't understand why You are letting me face this, but I will trust that You have a plan."

HE HEARS, HE DELIVERS, HE GIVES JOY – YOUR JOB IS SIMPLY TO TRUST.

Daniel had to trust God if he was going to have a purposed heart. He did not know what the reaction of the prince of the eunuchs would be. He had no idea the consequences that may have arisen because of his choice – He had to trust that God was in control. Daniel wanted to eat different food than what had been prescribed; he wanted to be allowed to follow a different set of rules. He had to trust that God would work out the details.

Sometimes the world tells us, "You have to have a great career; you have to make more money to provide for your family." But the world doesn't understand that you have a God who knows how to provide all that you need. Sometimes the world says, "You have a right to be bitter. Look at the situations you've gone through in life." But the world doesn't understand that we have a God who can give joy despite our circumstances. Don't fall for the world's lies. You can trust that God will handle every circumstance because of who He is.

2 - Make God Your Strength

Lo, this is the man that made not God his strength; but trusted in the abundance of his riches, and strengthened himself in his wickedness. (Psalm 52:7)

Made is the same Hebrew root word as *purposed.*

This principle is stated in the negative. Here we see what happens when you don't make God your strength. When you decide: "I can handle my problems on my own"; "I can decide the choices that seem best for me"; "I can handle this."

What do your actions look like when you don't make God your strength? God tells us in verses 2-4:

> *(2) The tongue deviseth mischiefs; like a sharp razor, working deceitfully. (3) Thou lovest evil more than good; and lying rather than to speak righteousness. Selah. (4) Thou lovest all devouring words, O thou deceitful tongue.*

(v. 2) Your tongue starts getting you in trouble when you decide you can handle your problems by yourself. Have you ever relied on your feelings about a situation and ended up saying something that you later regretted?

(v. 3) You begin to love evil more than good – the more wrong choices you make, the harder it is to make the right choice.

(v.3-4) You begin lying. And sometimes it may not be lying in the sense that "I am lying to you about...," but rather lying to yourself: "I don't need to know what God says about this decision"; or even "Well, this is such a small choice, I'm sure God doesn't care what I do about this." It is so easy to lie to ourselves when we are faced with something we don't want to hear, or something we don't want to change in our lives.

What are the consequences of not making God your strength? Look at verses 5-6 & 8:

> *(5) God shall likewise destroy thee for ever, he shall take thee away, and pluck thee out of thy dwelling place, and root thee out of the land of the living. Selah. (6) The righteous also shall see, and fear, and shall laugh at him: (8) But I am like a green olive tree in the house of God: I trust in the mercy of God for ever and ever.*

God destroys and the righteous laughs at the circumstances of the one whose strength is not found in God. This laughter shows that the righteous man knows what the unrighteous is missing. Have you ever stood by as someone was making a decision that you knew would take him down the wrong path (maybe to lay out of church for a while because his schedule was so busy), and when things fell apart, you thought to yourself, "Ha! I knew that wasn't going to work! I knew that was the wrong decision!"? Have you ever given someone cause to look at your decisions and laugh in their mind because you're not relying on God's strength to get you through your circumstances? If you are truly standing in God's strength, you understand what the world is missing.

God is strength, and He wants to be your strength. He wants you to let Him handle your problems. To make God your strength is to have the confidence that you can do what He wants you to do. You can face this trial. You can make the right decision.

> *The name of the LORD is a strong tower: the righteous runneth into it, and is safe. (Proverbs 18:10)*

> *I can do all things through Christ which strengtheneth me. (Philippians 4:13)*

Look carefully at the end of Psalm 52:7:
> *Strengthened himself in his wickedness.*

He has hardened himself in sin; hardened himself to God. When you refuse to let God be your strength, you are making the opposite choice: to strengthen yourself in wickedness. You might say, "That's not me. I don't strengthen myself in wickedness; I haven't hardened myself in sin."

> *If I regard iniquity in my heart, the LORD will not hear me. (Psalm 66:18)*

This is an attitude of "I will continue in my sin"; "This sin is okay for me." When you have a sin that you won't confess and get out of your life, you are strengthening yourself in wickedness. Maybe regarding gossip, worry, bitterness, etc. you've thought: "This is just my personality; I can't change who I am."

God knows that we are sinners; but when we sin, He expects us to make it right. He does not allow us to hold on to certain sins because "It's just who I am"; or "You just don't understand what I've been through."

> *If we say that we have no sin, we deceive ourselves, and the truth is not in us. (I John 1:8)*

To say that "bitterness" is okay for you to hold on to because of your circumstances, is to say that it is not a sin for you to hold on to it. And God says that when you say you have no sin, you are lying to yourself. Remember one of the actions of the man who has not made God his strength – lying.

GOD DOES NOT ALLOW US TO HOLD ON TO CERTAIN SINS BECAUSE "IT'S JUST WHO I AM."

No matter what circumstances you are facing, no matter how difficult the decision may be, God can give you the strength to do right. Daniel didn't have to face the prince of the eunuchs on his own. God was with him and helped him do right. Yes, you can do right – because God doesn't expect you to do right in your own strength.

3 - Make God Your Hope

> *That they might set their hope in God, and not forget the works of God, but keep his commandments. (Psalm 78:7)*

Set is the same Hebrew root word as *purposed.*

What does it mean to set your hope on something? Hope is to cherish a desire with anticipation; to desire with expectation of obtainment or fulfillment; to expect with confidence.

> *For I know the thoughts that I think toward you, saith the LORD, thoughts of peace, and not of evil, to give you an expected end. (Jeremiah 29:11)*

> *Being confident of this very thing, that he which hath begun a good work in you will perform it until the day of Jesus Christ. (Philippians 1:6)*

> *And we know that all things work together for good to them that love God, to them who are the called according to his purpose. (Romans 8:28)*

God has a plan – an expected end – a purpose for everything that He allows in your life. Not that you will always enjoy the current trial, but you know that He has a desired result to bring about in your life through that trial. In every choice you have to make, you can look to God and expect Him to do what is right in your life. You don't have to understand it. You don't even have to like it. But you have the hope that He gives that He will accomplish His purpose in your life.

IT'S NOT ABOUT WHAT I DESIRE FOR MY LIFE, BUT WHAT DOES GOD DESIRE FOR MY LIFE.

We like the beginning of Romans 8:28 "all things work together for good." But the end of that verse is just as important: "According to His purpose." It's not about what I desire for my life, but what does God desire for my life.

How do we make God our hope? Sometimes we know that God has a plan, and we know that He is working to bring about His desired result in our lives, but in the midst of the trial it can be hard to find that hope in God.

Notice Psalm 78:1-6, and then verse 7:

(1) Give ear, O my people, to my law: incline your ears to the words of my mouth. (2) I will open my mouth in a parable: I will utter dark sayings of old: (3) Which we have heard and known, and our fathers have told us. (4) We will not hide them from their children, shewing to the generation to come the praises of the LORD, and his strength, and his wonderful works that he hath done. (5) For he established a testimony in Jacob, and appointed a law in Israel, which he commanded our fathers, that they should make them known to their children: (6) That the generation to come might know them, even the children which should be born; who should arise and declare them to their children: (7) That they might set their hope in God, and not forget the works of God, but keep his commandments.

Remember what God has done for you. Spend time talking about how He is working in your life. Share the blessings He has given to you with others. Find someone to tell when God does something for you. Make sure your children know when God has provided or answered a prayer.

One of the things that I have found that has helped me is to keep a prayer journal. Every week I start by writing out the things I am praying for. I include myself, my family, my friends, my church, and my ministries. I add missionary families and government officials. As I go through the week, I will add prayer requests that come to my attention during that time – some for myself and some for people that I know. I write down the big things I am praying for and the little things I am praying for. Some things are needs, and some things are desires. Every time God answers a prayer, I draw a star next to that request. At the end of each week, I can look back to see what God has done for me. I can see how many times He has worked in my life; how many needs He has met; how many times He has been there to help me through my day. It's amazing to see how much time and care God puts into me – I know that He is working in my life, and He has a plan that is better than anything I could imagine.

When you reflect on what God has done for you this week, this month, this year, you can have hope that God will continue to work, though you may not see it or understand it.

If God is your hope, you can expect with confidence that He will work His good in your life. You can even anticipate and look forward to what He's doing.

4 - Make God Your Habitation

Because thou hast made the LORD, which is my refuge, even the most High, thy habitation. (Psalm 91:9)

Made is the same Hebrew root word as *purposed.*

Habitation is the act of inhabiting; occupation; a dwelling place.[vi] Verse 9 also mentions that the Lord *is my refuge.* Refuge is a shelter or protection from danger or distress.[vii]

Think for a moment about the life of Daniel. He truly found a refuge in God. Not only in Daniel chapter 1 was he given permission to abide by different rules that would allow him to follow God's laws, but all through the book of Daniel. Think of the time the king decided to kill all of his advisors because they could not tell him his dream and its interpretation. Daniel was one of the king's advisors. And yet, when Daniel prayed, God revealed the dream and interpretation to him so that he could give the king an answer. Remember Daniel chapter 6: "Daniel in the Lions' Den." God protected Daniel in times of danger and distress.

Make God your habitation. This dwelling is a place where you live. Think of this on the practical side for a moment. Your dwelling, where you live, is where your time is spent. It is where most of your concern is focused. Your life revolves around your home: you go to work, but you come back home; you can have a fun day of shopping, but you will come back home; you can go on the most amazing vacation of your life, but there is still something about just getting back home.

Home is where you are comfortable. You don't have to put on a special appearance. You don't have to worry about what someone might think: "She talks too much"; "She doesn't talk enough"; "I don't like the way she styles her hair"; "Did you see that color she was wearing?" At home, people know and accept you for who you are. They love you no matter how much you talk (I like to talk at home – a lot!) You are accepted even if the hairstyle didn't quite turn out the way you wanted!

YOU CAN NEVER TAKE A STAND IN YOUR DECISIONS FOR GOD, WITHOUT GOD.

We can be comfortable in God's presence. We don't have to worry about what He will think of our requests. We don't have to worry about being accepted by Him. He loves with an unconditional love and wants to see the very best for us. We can go to Him at any time, in any place, for any request. No request is too big or too small.

Casting all your care upon him; for he careth for you.
(I Peter 5:7)

Let us therefore come boldly unto the throne of grace, that we may obtain mercy, and find grace to help in time of need.
(Hebrews 4:16)

How do we make God our habitation, this special place where we get to dwell?

ABIDE:

He that dwelleth in the secret place of the most High shall
__abide__ under the shadow of the Almighty. (Psalm 91:1)

Abide in me, and I in you. As the branch cannot bear fruit
of itself, except it abide in the vine; no more can ye, except
ye abide in me. I am the vine, ye are the branches: He that
abideth in me, and I in him, the same bringeth forth much
fruit: for without me ye can do nothing. (John 15:4-5)

You will never have a purposed heart if you do not abide in Him. You can never take a stand in your decisions for God, without God.

SECRET PLACE:

He that dwelleth in the __secret place__ of the most High shall
abide under the shadow of the Almighty. (Psalm 91:1)

But thou, when thou prayest, enter into thy closet, and when
thou hast shut thy door, pray to thy Father which is in secret;
and thy Father which seeth in secret shall reward thee
openly. (Matthew 6:6)

Get alone with God in prayer. Spend time talking with Him – not just running through a prayer list really quickly so that you can fulfill your Christian duty. Ask Him for wisdom and direction. He never expects us to figure out the right choices on our own. He wants to give us His wisdom to help us.

> *If any of you lack wisdom, let him ask of God, that giveth to all men liberally, and upbraideth not; and it shall be given him. (James 1:5)*

If you faced a choice yesterday and asked God for His wisdom, you can still ask God for wisdom for the choices of today. His wisdom will never run out.

HIS TRUTH:

> *He shall cover thee with his feathers, and under his wings shalt thou trust: his truth shall be thy shield and buckler. (Psalm 91:4)*

How well do you know His truth? How well do you know the Word of God?

> *Thy righteousness is an everlasting righteousness, and thy law is the truth. (Psalm 119:142)*

> *Thou art near, O LORD; and all thy commandments are truth. (Psalm 119:151)*

> *Thy word is true from the beginning: and every one of thy righteous judgments endureth for ever. (Psalm 119:160)*

Get to know what God says in His Word. What would God say about that choice? What does the Bible say about witnessing, tithing, joy, peace, selfishness, worry, unforgiveness, anger? If there is something you are struggling with, take the time to find out what God says about that area. Making the decision God wants you to make starts with knowing what God says about that decision.

Are you comfortable in God's presence? Or are you in-and-out, stopping by for a quick visit every once in a while. If you had the time to just sit alone in a room with your Bible, and maybe your prayer journal, and spend time with God, how long could you sit there? Could you sit there for hours, having a conversation with your best Friend? Or would you just read the prescribed chapters for daily reading and rattle off your prayer list so that you could get on to other things?

CONCLUSION

Daniel purposed in his heart. He made a decision that required action to be able to keep it. It was not a one-time decision. This is not the type of decision that you make just once in your life and it sticks forever. It is a daily choice. Daniel went against the king's instructions, without thought of what everyone else was going to do, without giving in to fear.

THIS IS NOT THE TYPE OF DECISION THAT YOU MAKE JUST ONCE IN YOUR LIFE AND IT STICKS FOREVER. IT IS A DAILY CHOICE.

For Daniel to purpose in his heart, he had to trust that God was in control of the circumstances in which he found himself. Daniel knew that he could make the right choice because God would give him the strength to do so. Daniel's hope was in God; he had a confident expectation that God would answer him. Daniel made God his habitation. In every trial Daniel faced, you find him praying.

When Daniel made the right decision, he helped others make the right decision. We don't know if Shadrach, Meshach, and Abednego went with Daniel to talk to the prince of the eunuchs. It never says that they purposed in their hearts. But they followed Daniel's decision to not eat the king's meat. And God blessed all four of them for their decision to follow Him.

> *As for these four children, God gave them knowledge and skill in all learning and wisdom: and Daniel had understanding in all visions and dreams. (Daniel 1:17)*

Later, in Daniel chapter 3, Shadrach, Meshach, and Abednego stand up to the king and refuse to bow down to worship the golden image. Daniel is not found in chapter 3. At some point, these young men learned how to make the right decision without Daniel there to encourage them.

When you decide to take the right stand, you might help someone else to be able to do the same. There might be someone who is floundering and struggling, who is waiting on you to make the right decision. You might be the catalyst that helps them get to where they need to be.

Will you purpose in your heart to follow God? To make a daily decision to put these four things in your life so that when the time comes to make a choice, you will already have the tools you need to choose what is right?

If you are going to find refuge from this world – if you are going to keep your decisions for God – you must have a purposed heart.

Will you make God your trust? Your strength? Your hope? Your habitation?

If you will do these things daily, you will live with a purposed heart, ready for any decision that comes your way.

PART TWO

A UNITED HEART

Teach me thy way, O LORD; I will walk in thy truth: unite my heart to
fear thy name. (Psalm 86:11)

Throughout the book of Psalms, we find King David expressing himself to God in prayer, and we can catch a glimpse of the character of David.

Confession of sin:

> *(3) For I acknowledge my transgressions: and my sin is ever*
> *before me. (4) Against thee, thee only, have I sinned, and*
> *done this evil in thy sight: that thou mightest be justified*
> *when thou speakest, and be clear when thou judgest. (9) Hide*
> *thy face from my sins, and blot out all mine iniquities. (10)*
> *Create in me a clean heart, O God; and renew a right spirit*
> *within me. (Psalm 51:3-4, 9-10)*

Continual prayer:

> *Evening, and morning, and at noon, will I pray, and cry*
> *aloud: and he shall hear my voice. (Psalm 55:17)*

Trust despite fear:

> *(1) Be merciful unto me, O God: for man would swallow me up; he fighting daily oppresseth me. (2) Mine enemies would daily swallow me up: for they be many that fight against me, O thou most High. (3) What time I am afraid, I will trust in thee. (4) In God I will praise his word, in God I have put my trust; I will not fear what flesh can do unto me.*
> *(Psalm 56:1-4)*

Praise to God:

> *(1) O sing unto the LORD a new song; for he hath done marvellous things: his right hand, and his holy arm, hath gotten him the victory. (4) Make a joyful noise unto the LORD, all the earth: make a loud noise, and rejoice, and sing praise. (5) Sing unto the LORD with the harp; with the harp, and the voice of a psalm. (Psalm 98:1, 4-5)*

Love for God's Word:

> *O how I love thy law! it is my meditation all the day.*
> *(Psalm 119:97)*

Love for God's House:

> *I was glad when they said unto me, Let us go into the house of the LORD. (Psalm 122:1)*

Psalm 86 is a prayer of King David, and in the middle of this chapter David asks God to "unite my heart." What was David asking God for? He was certainly a man who loved and followed God. He spent much time in prayer and his requests were purposeful. He did not ask God for things by accident. So why this specific request? What work did David want God to accomplish through this prayer?

Unite means "to make to agree or be uniform; to join in interest or fellowship." In this verse in particular, it conveys the idea "to cause all its powers and affections to join with order and delight in the same objects."[viii]

David wanted his heart – his character, mind, and thinking – to agree with God. He wanted the objects of his desire to be what God wanted for his life, not simply what he wanted. In Psalm 40:8, David writes: "I delight to do thy will, O my God: yea, thy law is within my heart." David did not want to live a life in which he simply obeyed God; he wanted to follow God because of a desire to agree with God.

DAVID WANTED HIS HEART – HIS CHARACTER, MIND, AND THINKING – TO AGREE WITH GOD.

We see in the Bible that David's life was not free from sin and heartache. He was not a perfect man - he sinned with Bathsheba by committing adultery with her and murdering her husband to try to cover it up (II Samuel 11). He faced great struggles, such as when his wives were taken captive from Ziklag, and his own men wanted to stone him because of the destruction and captivity of their wives and children (I Samuel 30). Even his own son Absalom plotted against him (II Samuel 15). He fought many battles, the first of which is one of the most famous stories in the Bible:

David and Goliath (I Samuel 17).

In Acts 13:22, God refers to David as "a man after mine own heart, which shall fulfill all my will." How did David get to be this kind of man? A man that God would recognize as having a heart after His own? A man whose request for his heart to be united to fear God's name would most definitely be answered?

1 - What Does A United Heart Look Like

A UNITED HEART HAS CHOSEN ONE DIRECTION:

No man can serve two masters: for either he will hate the one, and love the other; or else he will hold to the one, and despise the other. Ye cannot serve God and mammon. (Matthew 6:24)

You are going to have to make a choice. If you are going to have a united heart, you cannot serve God one day and the world the next day. You cannot be faithful to God's commandments while you are at church, but live according to your own desires when you are at home.

A UNITED HEART IS "NOT A DIVIDED AND DISTRACTED HEART, AN HEART DIVIDED BETWEEN GOD AND THE WORLD, BETWEEN THE FEAR OF GOD AND THE FEAR OF MAN; BUT A HEART UNITED TO THE LORD, THAT CLEAVES TO HIM, AND HIM ONLY; A SINGLE AND A SINCERE HEART; A HEART THAT HAS A SINGLE VIEW TO

HIS GLORY, AND A SINGLE AFFECTION FOR HIM." (GILL)[IX]

You must make a final decision in your life, draw a line that you will never erase: I am following God with one hundred percent of my life. No matter what anyone else says or does. No matter the defeats you endure or the victories you gain.

YOU MUST MAKE A FINAL DECISION IN YOUR LIFE, DRAW A LINE THAT YOU WILL NEVER ERASE: I AM FOLLOWING GOD WITH ONE HUNDRED PERCENT OF MY LIFE.

The apostle Paul gives us an excellent example of this principle. Once Paul accepted Jesus Christ in Acts 9, he never again went back to his old life. Jesus had made Paul a new creation, and Paul spent the rest of his life wholly following God. He didn't serve God only when it was convenient. He didn't serve God only when it made sense. He didn't serve God only when God blessed. He served during the trials. He served despite the hardships and the persecution.

(23) Are they ministers of Christ? (I speak as a fool) I am more; in labours more abundant, in stripes above measure, in prisons more frequent, in deaths oft. (24) Of the Jews five times received I forty stripes save one. (25) Thrice was I beaten with rods, once was I stoned, thrice I suffered shipwreck, a night and a day I have been in the deep; (26) In journeyings often, in perils of waters, in perils of robbers, in perils by mine own countrymen, in perils by the heathen,

in perils in the city, in perils in the wilderness, in perils in
the sea, in perils among false brethren; (27) In weariness
and painfulness, in watchings often, in hunger and thirst, in
fastings often, in cold and nakedness.
(II Corinthians 11:23-27)

How could Paul experience all of these trials, yet continue to serve God? He had made a decision to know God: His power and His suffering. Nothing was going to stop Paul from living his life for God.

(7) But what things were gain to me, those I counted loss
for Christ. (8) Yea doubtless, and I count all things but
loss for the excellency of the knowledge of Christ Jesus my
Lord: for whom I have suffered the loss of all things, and
do count them but dung, that I may win Christ, (9) And be
found in him, not having mine own righteousness, which is
of the law, but that which is through the faith of Christ, the
righteousness which is of God by faith: (10) That I may know
him, and the power of his resurrection, and the fellowship of
his sufferings, being made conformable unto his death; (11)
If by any means I might attain unto the resurrection of the
dead. (12) Not as though I had already attained, either were
already perfect: but I follow after, if that I may apprehend
that for which also I am apprehended of Christ Jesus. (13)
Brethren, I count not myself to have apprehended: but this
one thing I do, forgetting those things which are behind, and
reaching forth unto those things which are before, (14) I

press toward the mark for the prize of the high calling of God in Christ Jesus. (Philippians 3:7-14)

What would it take to make you miss a day of Bible reading? A crazy day with the kids running you ragged, a long day at work, daily worries and frustrations? What would keep you from attending church on Sunday? An exhausting week at work, a family get-together, a person's unkind words at the last service? What would it take to get you to stop serving God completely? A financial setback, a health crisis, a relationship disappointment, the betrayal of a friend, a broken marriage, the loss of a loved one? Decide to follow God no matter what circumstances He allows you to face.

A UNITED HEART IS FOCUSED ON GOD:

My heart is fixed, O God, my heart is fixed: I will sing and give praise. (Psalm 57:7)

Your focus must be on God, not on the allures of the world, not on the desires of the flesh. Our hearts very easily lead us astray. David understood this principle. It only took one moment of focus on his own desires to bring about his sin with Bathsheba. He had to confess and make things right with God, and refocus his attention on what God desired for him, and not his own wants. Psalm 51 is David's prayer of confession after his sin. He expressed his desire for God to cleanse his heart.

Create in me a clean heart, O God; and renew a right spirit within me. (Psalm 51:10)

"OUR HEARTS ARE APT TO WANDER AND HANG LOOSE; THEIR POWERS AND FACULTIES WANDER AFTER A THOUSAND FOREIGN THINGS; WE HAVE THEREFORE NEED OF GOD'S GRACE TO UNITE THEM, THAT WE MAY SERVE GOD WITH ALL THAT IS WITHIN US, AND ALL LITTLE ENOUGH TO BE EMPLOYED IN HIS SERVICE... LET MY HEART BE FIXED FOR GOD, AND FIRM AND FAITHFUL TO HIM, AND FERVENT IN SERVING HIM; THAT IS A UNITED HEART." (HENRY)[x]

God appeared one night to King Solomon, David's son, in a dream. God said that Solomon could make a request, and God would grant it to him. Solomon chose to ask for wisdom. Pleased with Solomon's choice, God gave him not only great wisdom, but also long life, peace, and riches (I Kings 3). How is it then that Solomon, in his later years, would say:

(4) I made me great works; I builded me houses; I planted me vineyards: (5) I made me gardens and orchards, and I planted trees in them of all kind of fruits: (6) I made me pools of water, to water therewith the wood that bringeth forth trees: (7) I got me servants and maidens, and had servants born in my house; also I had great possessions of great and small cattle above all that were in Jerusalem before me: (8) I gathered me also silver and gold, and the peculiar treasure of kings and of the provinces: I gat me men singers and women singers, and the delights of the sons of men, as musical instruments, and that of all sorts. (9) So I was great, and increased more than all that were before me in Jerusalem:

also my wisdom remained with me. (10) And whatsoever mine
eyes desired I kept not from them, I withheld not my heart
from any joy; for my heart rejoiced in all my labour; and this
was my portion of all my labour. (11) Then I looked on all the
works that my hands had wrought, and on the labour that I
had laboured to do: and, behold, all was vanity and vexation
of spirit, and there was no profit under the sun.
(Ecclesiastes 2:4-11)

Looking back on his life and all that he had acquired and accomplished, Solomon said it was vanity – empty. He acknowledged his work and his riches. He even realized that he still had all the wisdom that God had given him. How then could his life be empty?

(1a) But Solomon loved many strange women... (3) And he
had seven hundred wives, princesses, and three hundred
concubines: and his wives turned away his heart. (4) For it
came to pass, when Solomon was old, that his wives turned
away his heart after other gods: and his heart was not perfect
with the LORD his God, as was the heart of David his father.
(I Kings 11:1a, 3-4)

Solomon had allowed his heart to be turned away from God. He allowed his focus to turn from God to his own desires. He still loved God. He still had great wisdom. He tried to teach his son how to follow after God (Proverbs). But his heart had not completely belonged to God. He recognized that God should have been his whole focus.

> *Let us hear the conclusion of the whole matter: Fear God, and keep his commandments: for this is the whole duty of man. (Ecclesiastes 12:13)*

As you decide to go one direction in life – completely following God – you must also decide to keep your focus on Him. You will not have a heart committed to following God if you let the things of this world, the desires of your flesh, turn your focus from God.

A UNITED HEART FEARS GOD:

> *(39) And I will give them one heart, and one way, that they may fear me for ever, for the good of them, and of their children after them: (40) And I will make an everlasting covenant with them, that I will not turn away from them, to do them good; but <u>I will put my fear in their hearts, that they shall not depart from me.</u> (Jeremiah 32:39-40)*

TO FEAR GOD IS TO RECOGNIZE WHO GOD IS, AND HAVE A REVERENCE FOR HIS CHARACTER.

As part of God's judgment upon His people, the children of Israel had been taken captive into other lands. God said that when He brought them back to their land He would give them "one heart, and one way." God said that He would put His fear into their hearts so that they would not turn their back on Him again.

If you are going to have a heart that agrees with God, you must fear Him. In Psalm 86, David asks God to unite his heart to fear God's name. To fear God is to recognize who God is, and have a reverence for His character. David understood God's judgment and His mercy.

> *For thou, Lord, art good and ready to forgive, and plenteous in mercy unto all them that call upon thee. (Psalm 86:5)*

Isaiah tells us that the seraphims in heaven fly around God's throne, praising Him for His holiness. When Isaiah recognized God's holiness, it called him to two actions: recognition and confession of who he was, and a surrender to God's will.

> *(3) And one cried unto another, and said, Holy, holy, holy, is the LORD of hosts: the whole earth is full of his glory. (4) And the posts of the door moved at the voice of him that cried, and the house was filled with smoke. (5) Then said I, Woe is me! for I am undone; because I am a man of unclean lips, and I dwell in the midst of a people of unclean lips: for mine eyes have seen the King, the LORD of hosts. (8) Also I heard the voice of the Lord, saying, Whom shall I send, and who will go for us? Then said I, Here am I; send me.*
> *(Isaiah 6:3-5, 8)*

A proper fear of God will always bring us to a place of action. How could we understand who God is, yet refuse to follow Him? How could we accept His salvation, yet not accept His leadership?

The phrase the fear of the Lord is found several times in the Bible, but here are just a few examples:

> *The fear of the LORD is the beginning of wisdom: a good understanding have all they that do his commandments: his praise endureth forever. (Psalm 111:10)*

> *The fear of the LORD is the beginning of knowledge: but fools despise wisdom and instruction. (Proverbs 1:7)*

> *The fear of the LORD is to hate evil: pride, and arrogancy, and the evil way, and the froward mouth, do I hate. (Proverbs 8:13)*

> *By mercy and truth iniquity is purged: and by the fear of the LORD men depart from evil. (Proverbs 16:6)*

> *Let not thine heart envy sinners: but be thou in the fear of the LORD all the day long. (Proverbs 23:17)*

If you fear God, you will have understanding and do His commandments; you will not despise instruction; you will hate evil; you will depart from evil; you will not envy sinners.

What does a united heart look like? It is a heart that has chosen to follow God's direction, that keeps its focus on God, and that fears God.

2 - How Do I Have A United Heart

In Psalm 86:11 when David asks God to unite his heart, he makes two simple statements of action. These actions will help us have the necessary tools to have a united heart.

RECEIVE KNOWLEDGE:

Teach me thy way, O LORD; (Psalm 86:11a)

If your heart is going to agree with God, you must know what God says. What does God say about marriage? About raising children? About church attendance? About finances? About music? About modesty? This list could go on.

Notice that David says, "Thy way." It doesn't matter what you want, think, or feel. What does God say? The Bible is all-sufficient: it has every answer for every question you have; every solution for every problem you face.

There are three simple things you can do to receive knowledge from God. First, you must read and study God's Word for yourself.

As newborn babes, desire the sincere milk of the word, that ye may grow thereby: (I Peter 2:2)

But his delight is in the law of the LORD; and in his law doth he meditate day and night. (Psalm 1:2)

Search the scriptures; for in them ye think ye have eternal life: and they are they which testify of me. (John 5:39)

Let the word of Christ dwell in you richly in all wisdom; teaching and admonishing one another in psalms and hymns and spiritual songs, singing with grace in your hearts to the Lord. (Colossians 3:16)

For the word of God is quick, and powerful, and sharper than any twoedged sword, piercing even to the dividing asunder of soul and spirit, and of the joints and marrow, and is a discerner of the thoughts and intents of the heart. (Hebrews 4:12)

As you read the Word of God, the Holy Spirit can speak to you. One of the jobs of the Holy Spirit is to teach you from God's Word. God wants you to know and understand His Word.

But the Comforter, which is the Holy Ghost, whom the Father will send in my name, he shall teach you all things, and bring all things to your remembrance, whatsoever I have said unto you. (John 14:26)

Howbeit when he, the Spirit of truth, is come, he will guide you into all truth: for he shall not speak of himself; but

whatsoever he shall hear, that shall he speak: and he will
show you things to come. (John 16:13)

Determine to read your Bible every day. If you are a new Christian, I would suggest that you start with the book of John or the gospels (the first four books of the New Testament). Read about how Jesus lived His life here on this earth. What did He do? How did He treat people?

If you have been faithfully reading your Bible for a while, you should be growing in your Bible reading. If you are consistently reading ten minutes a day, increase the time you spend in the Bible – even if it's just five more minutes. If you are reading one chapter a day, increase it to two chapters. None of us have arrived. We all still need to grow in the area of personal Bible reading.

Study to show thyself approved unto God, a workman that
needeth not to be ashamed, rightly dividing the word of truth.
(II Timothy 2:15)

Studying the Word of God is important to growing in your knowledge of Him. Maybe you read your Bible daily, but personal study is new for you. If you're not sure where to begin, you can start with three things: your Bible, a notebook, and a dictionary. As you read a passage of Scripture and you come across a word you don't fully understand, or even just want to know more about, look it up in the dictionary. In your notebook, take the time to write out the verse that God has brought to your attention. Then write out the definitions of the words in that verse. Oftentimes, simply having a greater understanding of the meaning of a word will help you to more fully understand the principle God wants you to learn from that verse.

THE GREATEST TOOL YOU WILL HAVE IN STUDYING THE WORD OF GOD WILL ALWAYS BE THE BIBLE ITSELF.

If you want to dig deeper in God's Word, talk to your pastor about finding trusted sources to help you. For example, sometimes understanding more about Bible customs will help you understand the actions of the Bible characters in a particular situation. There have been some great Bible teachers that have done a lot of work in writing out studies that can help you understand more difficult passages. In all resources, remember: they were written by man, and as such are capable of mistakes. Always compare what the study books say with the Word of God; if the study book doesn't agree with God's Word, God's Word is true. The greatest tool you will have in studying the Word of God will always be the Bible itself.

> *The judgments of the LORD are true and righteous altogether. (Psalm 19:9b)*

The first step to receiving knowledge from God is to read His Word.

Second, you must listen to Bible preaching.

> *(11) And he gave some, apostles; and some, prophets; and some, evangelists; and some, <u>pastors</u> and teachers; (12) <u>For the perfecting of the saints, for the work of the ministry, for</u>*

the edifying of the body of Christ: (13) Till we all come in
the unity of the faith, and of the knowledge of the Son of
God, unto a perfect man, unto the measure of the stature of
the fulness of Christ: (14) That we henceforth be no more
children, tossed to and fro, and carried about with every wind
of doctrine, by the sleight of men, and cunning craftiness,
whereby they lie in wait to deceive; (15) But speaking the
truth in love, may grow up into him in all things, which is
the head, even Christ: (16) From whom the whole body fitly
joined together and compacted by that which every joint
supplieth, according to the effectual working in the measure
of every part, maketh increase of the body unto the edifying
of itself in love. (Ephesians 4:11-16)

Preach the word; be instant in season, out of season; reprove,
rebuke, exhort with all longsuffering and doctrine.
(II Timothy 4:2)

Your pastor was given to you by God. His job is to preach the Word to help you learn and grow. The preaching of the Word of God will help to perfect you – make you mature in Christ. It will help you to grow in the ministry – serving Christ. Doctrine is simply teaching; what does God's Word teach about certain truths: the doctrine of the virgin birth, the doctrine of the second coming of Christ, the doctrine of God, the doctrine of the church. Part of the job of your pastor is to teach you what the Word of God says. This is a principle that we see the apostles following in the early church.

Then the twelve called the multitude of the disciples unto them, and said, It is not reason that we should leave the word of God, and serve tables. (4) But we will give ourselves continually to prayer, and to the ministry of the word.
(Acts 6:2, 4)

Third, to receive the knowledge of God, you can listen to godly counsellors. God doesn't expect us to know everything on our own. He gives us pastors to help teach us; but He also gives us people in our lives that can guide us.

The way of a fool is right in his own eyes: but he that hearkeneth unto counsel is wise. (Proverbs 12:15)

(20) Hear counsel, and receive instruction, that thou mayest be wise in thy latter end. (21) There are many devices in a man's heart; nevertheless the counsel of the LORD, that shall stand. (Proverbs 19:20-21)

Ointment and perfume rejoice the heart: so doth the sweetness of a man's friend by hearty counsel.
(Proverbs 27:9)

Notice the conditions of this counsel. Proverbs 19 tells us that the counsel should be of the Lord. In Proverbs 27, *hearty counsel* conveys the idea that it is healthy, sound counsel.[xi] Getting counsel is important, but make sure it is counsel that agrees with the Word of God. Beware of finding counselors that just tell you what you want to hear, not what God's Word says is right.

A godly counselor is one that will tell you the truth, even if it is hard to hear.

Faithful are the wounds of a friend; but the kisses of an enemy are deceitful. (Proverbs 27:6)

APPLY KNOWLEDGE:

I will walk in thy truth: (Psalm 86:11b)

Once you have received knowledge from God, the next step is to apply that knowledge. Here David says, "walk." To walk is to take repeated steps in the same direction. This requires consistent action: not a Sunday-only walk, but a daily walk. Determine every day to apply the Word of God to your life.

First, you must do what you learn. It is not enough to simply know what God teaches; you must then do what God teaches. When you learn a Bible principle, whether through personal reading, preaching, or counsel, you are responsible to do what you have been taught. Think of a time you taught someone how to do something: maybe you taught your child how to keep their room clean; maybe you taught someone at work how to input data in the computer. Did you expect that person to do what you had taught him, or did you expect him to listen and then do the opposite?

(24) Therefore whosoever heareth these sayings of mine and doeth them, I will liken him unto a wise man, which built his house upon a rock: (25) And the rain descended, and the floods came, and the winds blew, and beat upon that house;

and it fell not: for it was founded upon a rock. (26) And every one that heareth these sayings of mine, and doeth them not, shall be likened unto a foolish man, which built his house upon the sand: (27) And the rain descended, and the floods came, and the winds blew, and beat upon that house; and it fell: and great was the fall of it. (Matthew 7:24-27)

(22) But be ye doers of the word, and not hearers only, deceiving your own selves. (23) For if any be a hearer of the word, and not a doer, he is like unto a man beholding his natural face in a glass: (24) For he beholdeth himself, and goeth his way, and straightway forgetteth what manner of man he was. (25) But whoso looketh into the perfect law of liberty, and continueth therein, he being not a forgetful hearer, but a doer of the work, this man shall be blessed in his deed. (James 1:22-25)

Works are an outward expression of an inward belief. I believe God; therefore, I will do what He says. What is your attitude about "doing" after hearing the Word of God? Do you read the Bible with an attitude that says, "I know what God expects of me, but I just think..."; "I understand what God is teaching, but my personality..."? Do you listen to preaching with the thought: "Oh, I'm glad he's preaching on this topic. So-and-so really needs to hear this"? Do you just hear God's Word, or do you do God's Word?

When we do what God teaches in His Word, we show our faith to others.

(17) Even so faith, if it hath not works, is dead, being alone.
(18) Yea, a man may say, thou hast faith, and I have works:
shew me thy faith without thy works, and I will shew thee my
faith by my works. (James 2:17-18)

THE WORD OF GOD IN US KEEPS US WALKING THE RIGHT DIRECTION.

God says that we can have faith in Him, yet it can be dead – it is of no use in our life or to the lives of others. How can this be? Because when we don't use the faith that we have in Him through receiving knowledge, we are not truly walking with Him. We are not able to help others grow in their faith and knowledge of God. The Word of God in us keeps us walking the right direction.

The law of his God is in his heart; none of his steps shall
slide. (Psalm 37:31)

Second, allow God's Word to change you. How do we allow what we learn in God's Word to change our daily actions? Here are just a few examples:

I will set no wicked thing before mine eyes: I hate the work of
them that turn aside; it shall not cleave to me. (Psalm 101:3)

Bible principle: guard your eyes. Decide: I will be careful what I look at (television, internet, books, etc.).

Come and hear, all ye that fear God, and I will declare what
he hath done for my soul. (Psalm 66:16)

> *Hear; for I will speak of excellent things; and the opening of*
> *my lips shall be right things. (Proverbs 8:6)*

Bible principle: guard your ears. Decide: I will be careful what I will listen to. Does it uplift and glorify God? Is it excellent and right?

> *Finally, brethren, whatsoever things are true, whatsoever*
> *things are honest, whatsoever things are just, whatsoever*
> *things are pure, whatsoever things are lovely, whatsoever*
> *things are of good report; if there be any virtue, and if there*
> *be any praise, think on these things. (Philippians 4:8)*

> *Casting down imaginations, and every high thing that*
> *exalteth itself against the knowledge of God, and bringing*
> *into captivity every thought to the obedience of Christ;*
> *(II Corinthians 10:5)*

Bible principle: guard your mind. Decide: I will not allow my mind to dwell on temptations or things that would draw my focus away from God. I will keep my mind on what is right.

> *Let no corrupt communication proceed out of your mouth,*
> *but that which is good to the use of edifying, that it may*
> *minister grace unto the hearers. (Ephesians 4:29)*

Bible principle: guard your mouth. Decide: I will not curse. I will not gossip. I will use my words to build up and encourage others.

Test every action by the Word of God: what does the Bible say about what I see, hear, think, say? The more God teaches you, the more you can walk in His truth. The more you walk in His truth, the more united your heart will be to God's purpose.

CONCLUSION

David asked God to "unite my heart to fear thy name." God says that David was a man after God's heart – David lived his life in agreement with God's Word. This is what God desires for you. That you would live every day in accordance with the teachings of the Word of God.

If you are going to have a heart that agrees with God, you must choose to follow God completely – one direction, with your whole heart, no turning back. You must keep your focus on God: don't allow the cares or

TEST EVERY ACTION BY THE WORD OF GOD.

delights of the world to distract you from walking with God. You must fear God. Like Isaiah, recognize God's holiness; recognize who you are in light of God's character; surrender yourself completely to His will.

You can implement two actions every day that will help you have a united heart. Every day, receive knowledge from God. Get in His Word and let Him teach you. He will always direct you in the right way. Determine that as you learn from God, you will apply what you have learned; that you will carefully take repeated steps to follow after God.

Is your heart in agreement with God? If it is, don't quit. Keep walking with

God. If you're like me, you may have some areas that need to be addressed. What more can you learn from God? What steps can you take to walk closer to Him?

SALVATION

Having a purposed and united heart starts with a heart that knows Jesus Christ as Savior. It is God that helps us change our thinking and actions to live in agreement with Him, according to His purpose. You can never truly choose to follow God until you have first met Him as Savior. The first step in agreeing with God is to recognize your sinful condition and acknowledge that He is the only answer.

If you have never accepted Jesus Christ as your personal Savior, I would like to invite you to see what the Bible says about how you can know for sure that you are on your way to heaven.

RECOGNIZE YOUR CONDITION.

> *For all have sinned, and come short of the glory of God;*
> *(Romans 3:23)*

Every person on this earth is a sinner. This simply means that you do not measure up to God's holiness. As a sinner, there is nothing you can do to save yourself.

REALIZE THE PENALTY FOR SIN.

For the wages of sin is death; (Romans 6:23a)

God says that what you have earned for your sin is death. This death is an eternal separation from God in hell. Because your sin has earned you this punishment, there is no good deed that you can accomplish that will get you out of hell and into heaven.

BELIEVE CHRIST DIED AND ROSE FOR YOU.

But God commendeth his love toward us, in that, while we were yet sinners, Christ died for us. (Romans 5:8)

Knowing that Christ being raised from the dead dieth no more; death hath no more dominion over him. (Romans 6:9)

God loves you. One of the most famous verses in the Bible is John 3:16, "For God so loved the world, that he gave his only begotten Son, that whosoever believeth in him should not perish, but have everlasting life." God loves you so much that He sent His Son, Jesus Christ, to die on the cross in your place. When Jesus died for you, He paid the price for your sin. Three days after His death, Jesus Christ rose from the grave and is alive today. Because He conquered sin and death, He has the power to forgive you of your sin.

TRUST CHRIST ALONE AS YOUR SAVIOR.

For the wages of sin is death; but the gift of God is eternal life through Jesus Christ our Lord. (Romans 6:23)

(9) That if thou shalt confess with thy mouth the Lord Jesus, and shalt believe in thine heart that God hath raised him from the dead, thou shalt be saved. (10) For with the heart man believeth unto righteousness; and with the mouth confession is made unto salvation. (13) For whosoever shall call upon the name of the Lord shall be saved. (Romans 10:9-10, 13)

Salvation through Jesus Christ is a free gift. There is nothing you can do to earn God's forgiveness; He gives it freely to those who ask.

To confess means to say the same thing about yourself that God has said. God has said that you are a sinner, on your way to an eternity in hell. God said that the price for your sin has been paid by the shed blood of Jesus on the cross, and that He alone can offer forgiveness and a home in heaven. If you are willing to be honest and admit to God what He has already said, He has promised to give you salvation.

If you have never asked Jesus to be your Savior, but would like to do so now, He would love nothing more than to save you. You can call on Him in a simple prayer. Realize that the words themselves have no special powers, but it is your belief in what Jesus Christ has done for you that can save you.

SAMPLE PRAYER:

Dear Jesus, I know that I'm a sinner and deserving of hell. I know that there is nothing I can do to pay for my sin. I know that You died for me and rose again, and only You can save me. I trust You, and You alone to forgive my sin and give me a home in heaven. I ask you to be my Savior. Thank you for saving me. In Jesus name, Amen.

If you called on Jesus and asked Him to save you, then He promised in His Word that you have salvation. Romans 10:13 is a promise from God: "For whosoever [you can put your name in place of whosoever] shall call upon the name of the Lord shall be saved."

If you accepted Jesus as your Savior, we would like to rejoice with you in this decision. Please contact us at:

New Testament Baptist Church
1010 W. Grangeville Blvd. | Hanford, CA 93230
559.585.8464 | newtestamentbaptist.net

If you have any questions, we would love to help you. You can contact us at the previous information.

CITATIONS

i Strong, J. 7760 sum: purposed. https://www.blueletterbible.org/lexicon/h7760/kjv/wlc/0-1/

ii Ibid.

iii Merriam-Webster, "trust (noun 1)," accessed March, 2023, https://www.merriam-webster.com/dictionary/trust

iv Strong, J. 4409 mibtah: trust. https://www.blueletterbible.org/lexicon/h4009/kjv/wlc/0-1/

v words & music public domain

vi Merriam-Webster, "habitation (noun 1, 2)," accessed March, 2023, https://www.merriam-webster.com/dictionary/habitation vii Merriam-Webster, "refuge (noun 1)," accessed March, 2023, https://www.merriam-webster.com/dictionary/refuge

viii Websters Dictionary 1828, "unite (verb 3, 5)," accessed April, 2023, https://webstersdictionary1828.com/Dictionary/unite

ix Gill, John. John Gill's Exposition of the Bible., accessed February, 2023, http://www.biblestudytools.com/commentaries/gills- exposition-of-the-bible/psalms-86-11

x Henry, Matthew. Matthew Henry's Commentary on the Whole Bible., accessed February, 2023, http://www.biblestudytools.com/commentaries/matthew-henry-complete/Psalms/86

xi Websters Dictionary 1828, "hearty (adjective 2)," accessed April, 2023, https://webstersdictionary1828.com/Dictionary/hearty

Made in the USA
Las Vegas, NV
16 May 2023

72130846R00039